CONTENTS

Title page: Pacific King Prawns on Cocktail Sticks, page 12

Above: Turmeric Rice, page 74

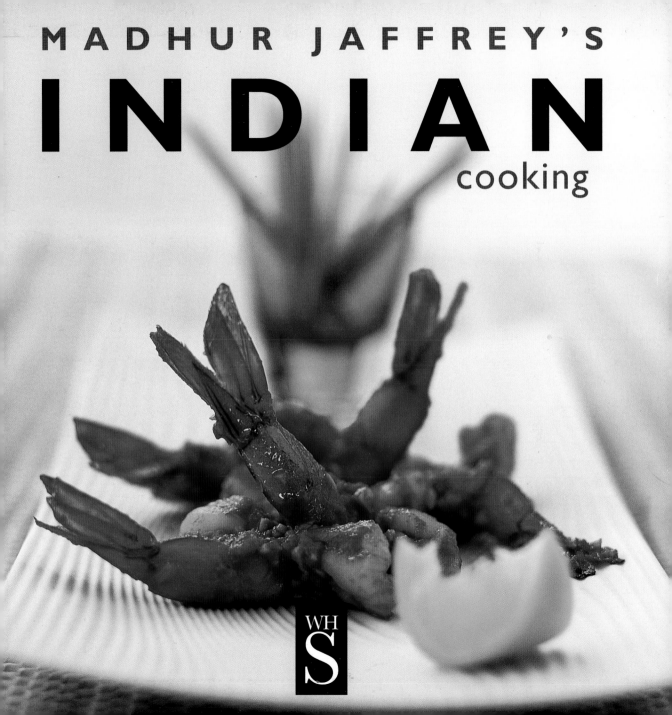

MADHUR JAFFREY'S
INDIAN
cooking

WHS

This edition first published in Great Britain in 2002 by Ebury Press
for WHSmith, Greenbridge Road, Swindon SN3 3LD

1 3 5 7 9 10 8 6 4 2

Ebury Press
Random House, 20 Vauxhall Bridge Road, London SW1V 2SA

Random House Australia (Pty) Limited
20 Alfred Street, Milsons Point, Sydney, New South Wales 2061, Australia

Random House New Zealand Limited
18 Poland Road, Glenfield, Auckland 10, New Zealand

Random House South Africa (Pty) Limited
Endulini, 5A Jubilee Road, Parktown 2193, South Africa

The Random House Group Limited Reg. No. 954009

www.randomhouse.co.uk

A CIP catalogue record for this book is available from the British Library.

Editor: Gillian Haslam
Designer: Christine Wood
Photographer: Craig Robertson
Food Stylist: Jules Beresford
Stylist: Helen Trent

ISBN 009188408X

Papers used by Ebury Press are natural, recyclable products made from wood grown in
sustainable forests.

Printed and bound in Italy by Graphicom srl.

INTRODUCTION

'Are there any Indian recipes that are quick and easy?' I am asked this question often. You have only to come to my house for dinner to know that there are – hundreds of them. You have to come during a weekday when I am also writing for 12–14 hours (or acting or gardening) and have barely time to sneeze. My husband and I eat well, even on those days.

Let's face it. There is no way to get instant marvellous food, but this book may help you come close. Some effort has to be expended in having a well-stocked larder and in some daily shopping. After that, there will be some chopping and stirring, but this can all happen, on the whole, within half an hour.

The secret lies in not being too ambitious. Have just a satisfying soup and salad for lunch, perhaps a vindaloo, plain rice and quickly stir-fried vegetables for dinner. For breakfast on Sundays, there are wonderfully spicy omelettes to be had, and for tea, how about onion fritters?

Do not be afraid to combine Indian main courses with Western side dishes: spicy fried fish with boiled potatoes and a green salad, an egg curry with toast. Indian breads are somewhat complicated to make, so get them from your local Indian restaurant or take-away or a supermarket to go with your home-made kebab or curry.

Also, do not be afraid of the long list of spices in some recipes. I have stayed away from dishes that require a lot of stirring or have too many steps. But stay away from too many spices? That would be like asking an Indian not to be Indian! If you can put one spice into a pan, you can just as easily put in ten or even fifteen of them. They will all cook quickly and easily.

With just a few exceptions, these recipes here can be prepared and cooked within 30 minutes. Although this calls for a pressure cooker in a small number of cases, its use is not essential. The cooking time will be longer without one, but the ingredients are quickly and easily prepared and the actual cooking methods are simple and trouble-free. Spices and seasonings are available from Indian grocers and many supermarkets. You may wish to remove some of the larger spices or whole chillies before serving. Follow one set of measurements only. Do not mix imperial and metric. Herbs, fruit juices, etc are fresh unless otherwise stated. Tablespoon measurements are level unless otherwise stated.

Chicken, Red Lentils and
Green Beans in One Pot,
page 48

STARTERS
and dips

GINGERY CAULIFLOWER SOUP

SERVES: 4–6   PREPARATION: 15 MINS   COOKING: 15 MINS

INGREDIENTS

3 tbsp vegetable oil

175 g (6 oz) onions, peeled and chopped

2.5 cm (1 in) piece fresh ginger, peeled and cut into fine slivers

4 cloves garlic, peeled and chopped

1 tsp ground cumin

2 tsp ground coriander

¼ tsp ground turmeric

⅛ –¼ tsp chilli powder

225 g (8 oz) potatoes, peeled and cut into rough 1 cm (½ in) dice

225 g (8 oz) cauliflower florets

1.2 litres (2 pints) chicken stock

salt if needed

150 ml (5 fl oz) single cream

NUTRITION

Each portion contains:

Energy: 150–290 calories

Fat: 11–16 g of which saturates 4–6 g

1 Set the oil over a highish heat in a good-sized saucepan. When the oil is hot and beginning to bubble, put in the onions, ginger and garlic. Stir and fry for about 4 minutes or until the onions start to turn brown.

2 Put in the cumin, coriander, turmeric and chilli powder. Stir once and put in the potatoes, cauliflower and chicken stock. If the stock is unsalted, put in ¾ tsp salt. Stir and bring to a boil. Cover, turn the heat to low and simmer gently for 10 minutes or until the potatoes are tender. Taste for salt, adding more if you like.

3 Put the soup into a blender, in 2 batches or more as required, and blend it thoroughly. Strain through a sieve, pushing down with a spoon to remove all the pulp. Add the cream and mix. Reheat the soup and serve.

COOK'S TIP

This soup may be served as an elegant first course or as part of a simple lunch. It may be made a day in advance and refrigerated before reheating. It is a good idea to have the cumin, coriander, turmeric and chilli powder all measured into a small bowl before you start as they go in together and cook very briefly.

CHICKEN LIVERS WITH FENNEL AND BLACK PEPPER

SERVES: 4–8   PREPARATION: 10 MINS   COOKING: 10 MINS

INGREDIENTS

¼ tsp ground turmeric

1 tsp ground cumin

1 tsp ground coriander

¼ tsp chilli powder

1 tbsp grainy French mustard

3 tbsp vegetable oil

¼ tsp fennel or anise seeds

10 fresh curry leaves, if available,
     or 3 bay leaves

3 cloves garlic, peeled and finely
     chopped

450 g (1 lb) chicken livers, each
     trimmed and separated into
     2 lobes

salt and freshly ground black pepper

120 ml (4 fl oz) single cream

3 tbsp finely chopped green
     coriander

NUTRITION

Each portion contains:

Energy: 143–285 calories

Fat: 10–21 g of which saturates 5–7 g

1 Put the turmeric, cumin, coriander, chilli powder and mustard into a small bowl with 2 tbsp water. Mix together well and set this spice paste aside.

2 Put the oil in a wok or a frying pan and set over a high heat. When the oil is hot and beginning to bubble, put in the fennel seeds, curry leaves and garlic. Stir and fry until the garlic turns golden.

3 Add the chicken livers. Sprinkle with ½ tsp salt and lots of black pepper. Stir and toss for 3–4 minutes or until nicely browned. Remove the livers with a slotted spoon and put in a serving dish or bowl.

4 Put the spice paste into the empty pan. Stir for 15 seconds or so. Add the cream and a light sprinkling of salt. Stir for 30–60 seconds or until the sauces thickens slightly. Pour the sauce over the chicken livers, sprinkle the green coriander over the top and serve.

COOK'S TIP

Cook these livers lightly so there is just a hint of pink inside them. You may serve them as a first course gor on toast as a snack.

PACIFIC KING PRAWNS ON COCKTAIL STICKS

SERVES: 4   PREPARATION: 15 MINS   COOKING: 10 MINS

INGREDIENTS

5 cloves garlic

2.5 cm (1 in) cube fresh root ginger

675 g (1½ lb) uncooked Pacific king prawns

3 tbsp vegetable oil

3 tbsp tomato purée

½ tsp ground turmeric

1 tbsp lemon juice

¾ tsp salt

⅛–¼ tsp cayenne pepper

NUTRITION

Each portions contains:

Energy: 81 calories

Fat: 1 g of which saturates 0.3 g

1 Peel and chop the garlic and ginger. Put them into an electric blender with 3 tbsp water and blend to a smooth paste.

2 Peel and de-vein the prawns (leave the tails on for decoration if you wish). Wash well and pat them dry. Cut each prawn into 3 pieces. Set aside.

3 Heat the oil in a 25–30 cm (10–12 in) frying pan over a medium heat. When the oil is hot and beginning to bubble, pour in the paste from the blender and fry, stirring constantly, for 2 minutes.

4 Add the tomato purée and the turmeric. Fry and stir for a further 2 minutes. Add 4 tbsp water, the lemon juice, salt and cayenne pepper. Cover and simmer gently for 2–3 minutes.

5 Lift off the cover, put in the prawns and turn the heat to high. Stir and fry the prawns for about 5 minutes or until they just turn opaque. Transfer to a serving platter with a container of cocktail sticks to insert into each prawn piece. Serve hot, with pappadums if you like.

COOK'S TIP

These spicy prawns make an excellent appetizer with drinks. Alternatively, double the quantities and serve without cocktail sticks as a main dish.

SPICY VEGETABLE FRITTERS

SERVES: 6–8 PREPARATION: 10 MINS COOKING: 15–20 MINS

INGREDIENTS

For the batter:

115 g (4 oz) chickpea flour (also
   called gram flour or besan)

¼ tsp salt

¼ tsp ground turmeric

¼ tsp ground cumin

¼ tsp bicarbonate of soda

⅛ tsp freshly ground black pepper

⅛ tsp cayenne pepper (optional)

For the filling:

3 medium potatoes, peeled (or
   other vegetables, see Cook's Tip)

vegetable oil for frying

salt and freshly ground black pepper

NUTRITION

Each portion contains:

Energy: 175–234 calories

Fat: 9–12 g of which saturates 1–1.5 g

1 To make the batter, sift the chickpea flour into a bowl. Gradually mix in about 200 ml (7 fl oz) water to make a batter thick enough to coat the vegetables. Add the other batter ingredients and mix well.

2 Cut the potatoes into thin rounds, 2 mm (⅛ in) thick, and immerse them in a bowl of cold water.

3 Pour oil into a wok or frying pan to a depth of 6.5–7.5 cm (2½–3 in) in the centre. Place on a low heat until hot but not smoking.

4 Take a few potato slices at a time, wipe them dry, and dip them in the batter. Now drop them into the oil, making sure they don't stick together. Fry slowly for 7–10 minutes on each side, until they are golden brown and cooked through.

5 Remove with a slotted spoon and drain on kitchen paper. Sprinkle with salt and pepper and keep hot while cooking the rest of the fritters in the same way. Serve while they are crisp and hot.

COOK'S TIP

Potatoes are specified here, but cauliflower florets, onion rings and pepper quarters are equally good. Serve with a dip or chutney.

See full picture on page 16.

ONION FRITTERS

SERVES: 6   PREPARATION: 10 MINS, PLUS STANDING TIME

COOKING: 7–8 MINS

INGREDIENTS

1 large egg

1 tbsp lemon juice

100 g (3½ oz) chickpea flour (also
    called gram flour or besan)

¾ tsp salt

½ tsp chilli powder

½ tsp garam masala

½ tsp cumin seeds

1 tsp ground cumin

¼ tsp ground turmeric

1 fresh, hot green chilli, de-seeded
    and finely chopped

2 tbsp chopped green coriander

vegetable oil for deep-frying

200 g (7 oz) onions, peeled and
    chopped into medium-sized dice

NUTRITION

Each portion contains:

Energy: 180 calories

Fat: 13 g of which saturates 2 g

1 Break the egg into a bowl and beat well. Add 4 tbsp water and the lemon juice. Mix. Add all the chickpea flour and mix well with a whisk. Put in the salt, chilli powder, garam masala, cumin seeds, ground cumin, turmeric, green chilli and green coriander. Mix well and set aside for at least 10 minutes or longer. Mix again with a whisk. The batter should be of a fairly thick, droppable consistency.

2 Put the oil in a wok or deep-fryer and set over a medium heat. You should have at least 7.5 cm (3 in) oil in the centre of the wok. When the oil is hot and beginning to bubble, put the onions into the batter and mix. (This should always be done just before frying.)

3 Take a heaped teaspoon of the batter and drop it into the hot oil. Use all the batter this way. Stir and fry the fritters for 7–8 minutes or until golden-red. Remove with a slotted spoon and drain on paper towels. Serve hot, as soon as the fritters are made.

COOK'S TIP
Serve a green chutney with
these fritters.

See full picture on page 17.

EASY CHICKEN KEBABS

SERVES: 4   PREPARATION: 10 MINS, PLUS STANDING TIME

COOKING: 8 MINS

INGREDIENTS

4 boned, skinned chicken breasts
    (about 560 g/1¼ lb)

¾ tsp salt

2 tbsp lemon juice

3 tbsp natural yoghurt

1 tbsp chickpea flour (also called
    gram flour or besan)

1 tsp peeled, very finely grated
    fresh ginger

2 cloves garlic, peeled and crushed
    to a pulp

¼ tsp chilli powder

¼ tsp ground turmeric

½ tsp ground cumin

½ tsp garam masala

4 tbsp melted butter or vegetable
    oil for basting

NUTRITION

Each portion contains:

Energy: 315 calories

Fat: 20 g of which saturates 11 g

1 Cut the chicken into 2.5 cm (1 in) cubes. Put in a bowl. Rub with ½ tsp of the salt and the lemon juice.

2 Put the yoghurt into a separate small bowl. Add the chickpea flour and mix well. Now put in the remaining ¼ tsp salt, ginger, garlic, chilli powder, turmeric, cumin and garam masala. Mix well. Pour this mixture over the chicken pieces. Mix well and set aside for 15 minutes or longer (you could even leave it overnight in the refrigerator).

3 Pre-heat the grill. Thread the chicken pieces onto 4 skewers and balance the skewers on the raised edges of the grill rack. You could, as an alternative, spread the chicken pieces out on the grill tray. Baste with the melted butter or oil.

4 Grill about 10 cm (4 in) from the source of heat for 5 minutes, basting once during this time. Turn the chicken pieces over, baste again and grill for 2–3 minutes or until they are just cooked through. Serve immediately.

COOK'S TIP

You may serve these kebabs with drinks, as a first course or even as a light main dish with rice. The pieces of meat may be skewered before grilling or they may be just spread out on a grill tray.

PRAWNS WITH GARLIC AND CHILLIES

SERVES: 6–8   PREPARATION: 15 MINS   COOKING: 5 MINS

INGREDIENTS

450 g (1 lb) medium-sized,
   uncooked, unpeeled prawns,
   peeled, de-veined and washed,
   then patted dry

1/4 tsp ground turmeric

1/4 tsp chilli powder

4 tbsp vegetable oil

1/2 tsp black or yellow mustard seeds

5 cloves garlic, peeled and finely
   chopped

1 fresh, hot green chilli, de-seeded
   and finely chopped

1/2 tsp salt

2 tsp finely chopped green
   coriander or parsley

NUTRITION

Each portion contains:

Energy: 73–100 calories

Fat: 6–9 g of which saturates 0.9–1 g

1 Put the prawns in a bowl. Sprinkle the turmeric and chilli powder over them evenly and rub in.

2 Put the oil in a wok or large frying pan and set over a high heat. When the oil is hot and beginning to bubble, put in the mustard seeds. As soon as they begin to pop – this takes just a few seconds – put in the garlic. Stir until the garlic has turned golden. Add the green chilli and stir once or twice.

3 Put in the prawns. Stir and fry them over high heat until they just turn opaque. This will take 2–3 minutes. Sprinkle with salt and toss. Finally, sprinkle with the green coriander, toss again and serve.

COOK'S TIP

Prawns cook so fast that you will spend more time peeling and de-veining them. I like to do this ahead of time and then keep them, washed and patted dry, in a polythene bag in the refrigerator, just ready to be stir-fried. You may serve them as a main dish as well, serving three to four people.

FRESH TOMATO SALAD

SERVES: 4–6   PREPARATION: 10 MINS   COOKING: 5 MINS

INGREDIENTS

675 g (1½ lb) tomatoes

20–25 basil leaves

½ tsp salt and freshly ground black
    pepper

⅛–¼ tsp chilli powder

2 tbsp lemon juice

3 tbsp vegetable oil (I use a
    mixture of 2 tbsp peanut oil and
    1 tbsp mustard oil)

½ tsp cumin seeds

½ tsp black or yellow mustard
    seeds

NUTRITION

Each portion contains:

Energy: 70–103 calories

Fat: 6–9 g of which saturates 0.7–1 g

1 Cut the tomatoes into 5 mm (¼ in) slices and arrange in slightly overlapping layers on a large plate.

2 Tuck the basil leaves into the layers of tomatoes so that about three-quarters of each leaf is visible. Do this evenly so that the green and red are attractively distributed. Sprinkle the salt, black pepper, chilli powder and lemon juice over the tomatoes.

3 Put the oil in a small saucepan and set over a high heat. When the oil is hot and beginning to bubble, put in the cumin and mustard seeds. As soon as the mustard seeds begin to pop – this takes just a few seconds – lift the saucepan off the heat and spoon the oil and spices over the tomatoes. Serve immediately.

COOK'S TIP

This tastes best when tomatoes are in season. The addition of fresh basil leaves is a quirky preference of mine, mainly because they grow in such abundance in my garden and look so pretty. You could just as easily tuck in sprigs of fresh mint or green coriander.

FRESH GREEN MANGO CHUTNEY

MAKES: 600 ML (1 PINT)   PREPARATION: 15 MINS, PLUS SOAKING TIME

COOKING: 45 MINS

INGREDIENTS

½ tsp fenugreek seeds

about 675–900 g (1½ –2 lb) green,
    unripe mango or mangoes

4 tbsp mustard oil (use olive oil as
    a substitute)

½ tsp cumin seeds

½ tsp fennel seeds

½ tsp black or yellow mustard seeds

¼ tsp kalonji seeds

6 cm (2½ in) piece fresh ginger,
    peeled and cut into fine strips

¼ tsp ground turmeric

1–1¼ tsp salt

5–6 tbsp sugar

3–4 fresh, hot green chillies,
    de-seeded and chopped

½ tsp chilli powder

NUTRITION

Each tablespoon/15ml contains:

Energy: 26 calories

Fat: 1 g of which saturates 0 g

1 Soak the fenugreek seeds in 6 tbsp water overnight. (Alternatively, put ¼ tsp fenugreek seeds into the hot oil with the cumin in step 3.)

2 Peel the mango and cut the flesh off the stone. Cut into strips 5 mm (¼ in) thick and wide and 5–7.5 cm (2–3 in) long. If you are in a rush, chop the flesh coarsely.

3 Set the oil over a highish heat. When the oil is hot, put in the cumin, fennel, mustard and kalonji seeds. As soon as the mustard seeds begin to pop – this takes just a few seconds – put in the ginger. Stir and fry it for 2 minutes or until it just starts to change colour.

4 Now put in the soaked fenugreek seeds with their soaking liquid as well as another 250 ml (8 fl oz) water and turmeric. Bring to the boil. Cover, lower the heat and simmer for 15 minutes.

5 Add the mango, salt, sugar, chillies and chilli powder. Stir to mix and bring to a simmer. Simmer, uncovered, on a medium-low heat for 25–30 minutes or until the chutney is thick and the mango pieces are translucent and tender. Serve at room temperature with pappadums.

COOK'S TIP

This will keep in a closed jar in the fridge for a couple of weeks. For hotter chutney, increase the amount of chilli powder. Mangoes vary in sourness so taste 5 minutes before it is ready so you can adjust the sugar and salt. Kalonji seeds are small tear-shaped black seeds sold by Indian grocers.

DEEP FRIED PUFFY BREADS

SERVES: 3–4   PREPARATION: 10 MINS

COOKING: 5 MINS, PLUS 15–30 MINS RESTING TIME FOR THE DOUGH

INGREDIENTS

225 g (8 oz) chapati flour or a
   mixture of 115 g (4 oz) sieved
   wheatmeal flour and 115 g (4 oz)
   plain white flour

½ tsp salt

2 tbsp vegetable oil plus more for
   deep-frying

about 100–200 ml (3½ –4 fl oz)
   milk or water

NUTRITION

Each portion contains:

Energy: 350–470 calories

Fat: 18–24 g of which saturates 3–4 g

1 Put the flour in a bowl. Add the salt and mix it in. Dribble the 2 tbsp oil over the top and rub it into the flour with your fingers. Slowly add the milk or water to form a medium-soft ball of dough. Knead the dough for 10 minutes or until smooth. Form a smooth ball, rub it with a little oil and set it aside, covered with cling film, for 15–30 minutes.

2 Put enough oil for deep-frying into a wok or deep frying pan and set over a medium heat. As the oil heats, divide the dough into 12 balls. Roll one ball out into a 13 cm (5 in) round. Keep it covered with cling film. Roll out all the pooris this way and keep them covered.

3 When the oil is hot and beginning to bubble, lay one poori carefully over the surface of the oil without letting it fold up. It should sizzle immediately. Using the back of a slotted spoon, push the poori gently into the oil with quick strokes. It should puff up in seconds. Turn the poori over and cook on the other side for a few seconds.

4 Remove with a slotted spoon and keep on a large plate lined with paper towels. Make all the pooris this way and eat immediately.

COOK'S TIP

Chapati flour is sold by all Indian grocers. Poori is the Indian name for these breads. They are good served with chutney or dips.

MAIN
courses

LAMB STEWED IN COCONUT MILK

SERVES: 4   PREPARATION: 15 MINS   COOKING: 25 MINS

INGREDIENTS

3 tbsp vegetable oil

12 fresh curry leaves, if available,
    or 3 bay leaves

5 cm (2 in) cinnamon stick

6 cardamom pods

8 cloves

15 black peppercorns

85 g (3 oz) onions, peeled and
    chopped

675 g (1½ lb) boned shoulder of
    lamb, cut into 4 cm (1½ in)
    chunks

450g (1 lb) potatoes, peeled and
    cut into pieces the same size as
    the meat

2 medium-sized carrots, peeled and
    cut into 3 pieces each

¼ tsp ground turmeric

1 tbsp ground coriander

⅛–½ tsp chilli powder

1–2 fresh, hot green chillies,
    de-seeded and chopped

1¼ tsp salt

one 400 g (14 oz) tin coconut milk,
    well stirred

1 Put the oil in a pressure-cooker and set over a medium-high heat. When the oil is hot and beginning to bubble, put in the curry leaves, cinnamon, cardamom, cloves and peppercorns. Stir once and put in the onions. Sauté for 1½ minutes or until the onions are soft, and put in the meat, potatoes, carrots, turmeric, coriander, chilli powder, green chillies, salt and 250 ml (8 fl oz) of the coconut milk.

2 Cover securely with the lid and, on a high heat, bring to full pressure.

3 Turn the heat to low and cook for 15 minutes. Lower the pressure with the help of cool water and remove the lid. Cook, uncovered, over high heat for 5 minutes, stirring gently as you do this. Add the remaining coconut milk, bring to a simmer and then serve.

COOK'S TIP

This is a meal in itself requiring only rice or crusty bread on the side. I have used a pressure-cooker for speed. The cooking time in a saucepan would be about 70 minutes and you would need to add 150 ml (5 fl oz) water before starting to cook. This stew may be made up to a day ahead, then cooled and refrigerated before reheating the next day.

NUTRITION

Each portion contains:

Energy: 680 calories

Fat: 43 g of which saturates 24 g

SMOTHERED LAMB (OR PORK OR BEEF)

SERVES: 3–4   PREPARATION: 15 MINS   COOKING: 25 MINS

INGREDIENTS

450 g (1 lb) boned shoulder of lamb
    or pork shoulder or stewing beef,
    cut into 2.5 cm (1 in) cubes

115 g (4 oz) onions, peeled and
    finely chopped

2.5 cm (1 in) piece fresh ginger,
    peeled and finely chopped

140 g (5 oz) tomatoes, skinned and
    finely chopped

3 tbsp finely chopped green
    coriander

1–2 fresh, hot green chillies,
    de-seeded and cut into fine rings

¼ tsp ground turmeric

2 tsp garam masala

1 tsp ground cumin

4 tbsp natural yoghurt

1 tbsp tomato purée

¾ tsp salt or to taste

3 tbsp vegetable oil

4 cloves garlic, peeled and finely
    chopped

freshly ground black pepper

1 Put all the ingredients except the oil, garlic and black pepper into a bowl and mix well.

2 Put the oil in a pressure-cooker and set over a medium-high heat. When the oil is hot and beginning to bubble, put in the garlic. Stir until the garlic turns medium-brown.

3 Add the seasoned meat and stir once or twice. Turn the heat to medium. Cover the pressure-cooker tightly and bring up to pressure slowly. Cook lamb and pork for 15 minutes and beef for 20 minutes at full pressure.

4 Reduce the pressure quickly with the help of cool water. Uncover. Cook, uncovered, over a high heat until the sauce is thick, stirring gently as you do so. Sprinkle in lots of black pepper and stir again.

NUTRITION

Each portion contains:

Energy: 280–380 calories

Fat: 18–24 g of which

saturates 6–8 g

COOK'S TIP

There may be a number of ingredients here but they are added at almost the same time so preparation is quick. This dish can be cooked in a regular saucepan, but will take from 1 to 1½ hours (the longer time for beef) and you will need to add about 300 ml (5 fl oz) water just before you start to cook. Serve with rice.

BEEF OR LAMB WITH ONION AND GREEN PEPPER

SERVES: 3–4 PREPARATION: 15 MINS COOKING: 10 MINS

INGREDIENTS

340 g (12 oz) cooked, boneless
   roast beef or roast lamb
½ tsp freshly ground black pepper
¼–½ tsp chilli powder
1 tsp ground cumin
1 tsp ground coriander
¼ tsp ground turmeric
1 tsp red wine vinegar
salt
3 tbsp vegetable oil
½ tsp cumin seeds
½ tsp black or yellow mustard seeds
10 fenugreek seeds (optional)
115 g (4 oz) green pepper,
   de-seeded and cut, lengthways,
   into 3 mm (⅛ in) slivers
140 g (5 oz) onions, peeled and cut
   into fine half-rings
1 tsp Worcestershire sauce

NUTRITION

Each portion contains:

Energy: 280–370 calories

Fat: 19–25 g of which saturates 6–7 g

1 Cut the cooked meat into 5 mm (¼ in) slices. Now stack a few slices together at a time and cut into 5 mm (¼ in) slivers. This does not have to be done too evenly.

2 Combine the black pepper, chilli powder, cumin, coriander, turmeric, vinegar, ½ tsp salt and 2 tbsp water in a small cup. Mix together and set aside.

3 Put the oil in a large frying pan over a medium-high heat. When the oil is hot and beginning to bubble, add the cumin, mustard and fenugreek seeds. As soon as the mustard seeds begin to pop, put in the green pepper and onion. Stir and fry until the onion has browned quite a bit and the mass of vegetables has reduced. Sprinkle about ⅛ tsp salt over the top and stir.

4 Add the meat and the spice mixture from the cup. Stir rapidly on the same medium-high heat for a minute or so until the meat has heated through. Add the Worcestershire sauce and stir to mix. Serve immediately.

COOK'S TIP
One or two sliced green chillies may be added to at the same time as the green pepper if you want it really hot. Serve with rice, potatoes or breads. The meat is also excellent stuffed into pitta breads with shredded lettuce and sliced tomato.

BEEF OR LAMB WITH SPINACH

SERVES: 4   PREPARATION: 10 MINS   COOKING: 25–30 MINS

INGREDIENTS

285 g (10 oz) frozen chopped
    spinach
285 g (10 oz) onions, peeled and
    coarsely chopped
5 cm (2 in) piece fresh ginger,
    peeled and coarsely chopped
6–8 cloves garlic, peeled
6 tbsp vegetable oil
3 bay leaves
10 cardamom pods
8 cloves
two 5 cm (2 in) cinnamon sticks
600 g (1½ lb) stewing beef or
    boned shoulder of lamb, cut
    into 4 cm (1½ in) cubes
1⅓ tsp salt
1 tbsp ground coriander
1 tsp ground cumin
¼ –1 tsp chilli powder
½ tsp garam masala

NUTRITION

Each portion contains:

Energy: 370 calories

Fat: 24 g of which saturates 5 g

1 Drop the spinach in boiling water according to packet instructions and boil until defrosted. Drain and squeeze out most of the water.

2 Put the onions, ginger and garlic into a food processor and 'pulse', starting and stopping with great rapidity, until finely chopped.

3 Put the oil into a pressure-cooker and set over a high heat. When the oil is hot and beginning to bubble, put in the bay leaves, cardamom pods, cloves and cinnamon sticks. Stir once or twice and put in the finely chopped seasonings from the food processor. Stir and cook over high heat for 5 minutes.

4 Put in the beef or lamb, the spinach, 450 ml (15 fl oz) water, salt, coriander, cumin and chilli powder. Stir. Cover, securing the pressure-cooker lid, and bring up to full pressure. The beef will take 20 minutes, the lamb 15 minutes.

5 Cool off the pressure-cooker quickly with cool water and remove the lid. Put in the garam masala and bring the contents of the pressure-cooker back to the boil. Cook, uncovered, stirring gently over a high heat for about 7–10 minutes or until the sauce is reduced and thick. Skim off the oil with a spoon before serving.

COOK'S TIP

To make this classic dish quickly, a pressure-cooker is essential. If you use a regular saucepan it will take about 1 hour for lamb to cook and 1½ hours for beef. You will need to increase the amount of water to 600 ml (1 pint).

PORK OR LAMB VINDALOO

SERVES: 3–4   PREPARATION: 10 MINS   COOKING: 20 MINS

INGREDIENTS

1½ tbsp grainy French mustard

1½ tsp ground cumin

¾ tsp ground turmeric

½ –1 tsp chilli powder

1 tsp salt

1 tsp red wine vinegar

3 tbsp vegetable oil

115 g (4 oz) onions, peeled and cut
   into fine half-rings

6 large cloves garlic, peeled and
   crushed to a pulp

560 g (1¼ lb) boned hand of pork
   or shoulder of lamb, cut into
   2.5 cm (1 in) cubes

150 ml (5 fl oz) tinned coconut
   milk, well stirred

NUTRITION

Each portion contains:

Energy: 370–500 calories

Fat: 25–34 g of which saturates 11–14 g

1 Combine the mustard, cumin, turmeric, chilli powder, salt and vinegar in a cup. Mix well.

2 Put the oil in a large, non-stick frying pan and set over a medium-high heat. When the oil is hot and beginning to bubble, put in the onions. Stir and fry until they are medium-brown. Put in the garlic. Stir and fry for 30 seconds. Put in the paste from the cup. Stir and fry for a minute. Put in the meat. Stir and fry for about 3 minutes.

3 Transfer everything from the frying pan to a pressure cooker and add the coconut milk and 150 ml (5 fl oz) water. Cover and bring up to full pressure. Lower the heat to a simmer and cook for 20 minutes.

4 Cool off the pressure cooker quickly with cool water, remove the lid and serve.

COOK'S TIP

This dish may also be made in a frying pan, but you will need to add 250 ml (8 fl oz) of water and allow 1 hour or so of simmering. Whichever method you use, once the simmering starts the cook is off duty! Vindaloos are hot – Goans would use 4 tsp of chilli powder here. Under my husband's 'spare-me' gaze, I have made a mild dish. It is up to you.

EGGS WITH FRESH GREEN HERBS

SERVES: 2–4   PREPARATION: 10 MINS   COOKING: 5 MINS

INGREDIENTS

5 large eggs

salt and freshly ground black pepper

2 tbsp vegetable oil

3 spring onions, cut into fine
    rounds (the white as well as the
    green sections)

1 clove garlic, peeled and very
    finely chopped

3 tbsp finely chopped green
    coriander, plus some whole
    leaves to garnish

1–2 fresh, hot green chillies,
    de-seeded and sliced into fine
    rounds

2.5 cm (1 in) piece fresh ginger,
    peeled and very finely chopped

generous pinch of ground turmeric

1½ tsp lemon juice

⅓ tsp sugar

NUTRITION

Each portion contains:

Energy: 161–323 calories

Fat: 13–27 g of which saturates 3–6 g

1   Break the eggs into a bowl and beat well. Add a generous ¼ tsp salt and lots of freshly ground black pepper and set aside.

2   Put the oil in a large, non-stick frying pan and set over a medium-high heat. When the oil is hot and beginning to bubble, put in the spring onions. Stir and fry until the onions just start to brown at the edges. Put in the garlic and stir for a few seconds. Now put in the green coriander, chillies, ginger and turmeric. Stir for a few seconds.

3   Add the lemon juice and sugar and stir to mix. Working quickly, spread the herbs around evenly in the pan.

4   Now pour in the beaten eggs and let them spread to the edges of the pan. Cover, turn the heat to medium-low and cook for a few minutes, until the eggs have just set. Cut into wedges, garnish with fresh coriander and serve immediately.

COOK'S TIP

This may be served at breakfasts and brunches as soon as it comes out of the frying pan (I serve it with toast) and may also be sliced and put into sandwiches to perk up a picnic or an office lunch. It is really a kind of flat egg pancake seasoned with spring onions, green coriander, green chillies, ginger and garlic. It is a good idea to have everything cut and ready before you start as this dish cooks very quickly.

GARLICKY MUSHROOM 'MASALA' OMELETTE

SERVES: 2   PREPARATION: 10 MINS   COOKING: 5 MINS

INGREDIENTS

5 large eggs

salt and freshly ground black pepper

4 tbsp vegetable oil

½ tsp black or yellow mustard seeds

1 large clove garlic, peeled and very
    finely chopped

4 large or 6 medium-sized
    mushrooms, sliced lengthways

3 spring onions, cut into very fine
    rounds (the white as well as the
    green sections)

1 fresh, hot green chilli, de-seeded
    and cut into very fine rounds

4 heaped tbsp coarsely chopped
    green coriander

2.5 cm (1 in) piece fresh ginger,
    peeled and finely grated

4 tbsp tinned chopped tomatoes

NUTRITION

Each portion contains:

Energy: 450 calories

Fat: 39 g of which saturates 8 g

1 Break the eggs into a bowl. Add a generous ¼ tsp salt and some freshly ground black pepper and beat well. Pour into a jug and set aside.

2 Put 2 tbsp of the oil into a medium-sized frying pan and set over a high heat. When the oil is hot and beginning to bubble, put in the mustard seeds. As soon as they begin to pop – this takes just a few seconds – put in the garlic. Stir once or twice. As soon as the garlic starts to brown, put in the mushrooms and stir until the mushrooms lose their raw look.

3 Now turn the heat to medium and put in the spring onions, green chilli, green coriander and ginger. Stir until the green seasonings have wilted – about a minute. Put in the tomatoes and a little salt and pepper. Stir for about 30 seconds and turn off the heat. This is the omelette filling.

4 Put 1 tbsp of the oil into an 18 cm (7 in) non-stick or other omelette pan and set over a high heat. When the oil is hot and beginning to bubble, pour in half the beaten eggs. Using a wooden spoon or the back of a fork, stir the eggs for the next 3–4 seconds until they look like lumps of soft custard held together in one unbroken layer.

5 Quickly spread half the filling along the centre of the omelette and fold it over. Cook for another few seconds and flip the omelette over on to a warm plate.

6 Make the second one the same way and serve immediately.

SPICY GRILLED CHICKEN

SERVES: 4   PREPARATION: 5 MINS   COOKING: 20–25 MINS

INGREDIENTS

1.25 kg (2¾ lb) jointed chicken
  pieces

For the spice paste:

1 tbsp coarsely crushed black
  peppercorns

1 tbsp paprika (bright red, if
  possible)

½ tsp chilli powder or to taste

1 tbsp garam masala

2 tsp ground cumin

2 tsp oregano

1 clove garlic, peeled and crushed

1¼ tsp salt

3 tbsp vegetable oil

2 tbsp lemon juice

2 tbsp natural yoghurt

NUTRITION

Each portion contains:

Energy: 260 calories

Fat: 15 g of which saturates 3 g

1 Pre-heat the grill and arrange the grill tray at least 13–15 cm
  (5–6 in) from the source of heat. If you can control your heat, set it
  at medium-high.

2 Combine all the ingredients for the spice paste in a bowl and mix
  well. Rub the paste over the chicken as evenly as possible.

3 Arrange the chicken pieces on the grill tray in a single layer, with the
  fleshier parts up and the skin side down. Grill for 10–12 minutes or
  until browned. You may need to rearrange some of the pieces so that
  they all brown evenly. Turn the pieces over and cook the second side
  in the same way. Serve immediately.

COOK'S TIP

Most Indian grilled chicken dishes require a marinading period but if you are
rushed, follow this recipe and you will come up with delicious results – fast.
This chicken may be served, Western-style, with boiled potatoes and a green
vegetable or salad. You may also serve it with rice and an Indian vegetable.
The spice paste may be prepared up to a day ahead of time and refrigerated. You
can also rub the chicken pieces with the spice paste and leave them for up to
24 hours in the refrigerator before grilling.

CHICKEN IN A GREEN CORIANDER, SPINACH AND MUSTARD SAUCE

SERVES: 3–4   PREPARATION: 15 MINS   COOKING: 45 MINS

INGREDIENTS

4 tbsp vegetable oil

3 bay leaves

6 cardamom pods

5 cm (2 in) cinnamon stick

5 cloves

2 dried, hot red chillies

1 kg (2¼ lb) chicken pieces,
    skinned and cut into portions (a
    pair of breasts into 4–6 pieces
    each, whole legs into 2–3 pieces)

4 tbsp sultanas

6 tbsp natural yoghurt

salt and freshly ground black pepper

⅛–¼ tsp chilli powder

5 cm (2 in) piece fresh ginger,
    peeled and coarsely chopped

1–2 fresh, hot green chillies,
    de-seeded and chopped

generous fistful of green coriander
    tops (leaves and tender stems)

285 g (10 oz) frozen, chopped
    spinach, boiled until just
    defrosted, then lightly drained

3 tbsp grainy French mustard

1   Put the oil in a large, wide, non-stick pan and set over a medium-high heat. When the oil is hot and beginning to bubble, put in the bay leaves, cardamom pods, cinnamon stick, cloves and red chillies. Stir for a few seconds or until the bay leaves turn a few shades darker.

2   Add the chicken pieces and brown well on both sides. Put in the sultanas and stir for a few seconds. Now put in the yoghurt, 1 tsp salt, lots of freshly ground black pepper and the chilli powder. Stir and bring to a simmer. Cover well, turn the heat to low and simmer gently for 15 minutes.

3   While the chicken simmers, put the ginger into a blender along with 3 tbsp water and blend until you have a smooth paste. Coarsely chop the green chillies and add to the ginger with the green coriander and continue to blend, pushing down with a rubber spatula when necessary.

4   Add the drained spinach. Blend very briefly. The spinach should have a coarse texture and should not be a fine purée. Empty this green sauce into a bowl. Add the mustard and ¼ tsp salt. Mix.

5   When the chicken has cooked for 15 minutes, remove the cover and add the green sauce. Stir to mix. Bring to a simmer, cover again and cook for about 10 minutes or until the chicken is tender. Turn the chicken pieces a few times during this period. Serve immediately.

NUTRITION

Each portion contains:

Energy: 420–557 calories

Fat: 21–27 g of which saturates 5–6 g

COOK'S TIP

You can serve this superb dish as part of a grand Indian meal or, as I sometimes do, with mashed potatoes and grilled tomatoes. No other vegetable is needed as the sauce is almost entirely made up of spinach with the green coriander providing an extra dimension of flavour. Of course, you could always serve it with rice, plain boiled potatoes or bread.

CHICKEN, RED LENTILS AND GREEN BEANS IN ONE POT

SERVES: 4–6   PREPARATION: 10 MINS   COOKING: 45 MINS

INGREDIENTS

6 tbsp vegetable oil

3 bay leaves

5 cloves

6 cardamom pods

5 cm (2 in) cinnamon stick

3 dried hot red chillies

900 g (2 lb) chicken pieces, skinned, cut into smaller portions (a pair of breasts into 4–6 pieces each; whole legs into 2–3 pieces each)

285 g (10 oz) red lentils (masoor dal), picked over, washed and drained

½ tsp ground turmeric

salt and freshly ground black pepper

1½ tsp garam masala

1½ tbsp lemon juice

180 g (6 oz) green beans, trimmed into 2.5 cm (1 in) lengths

generous pinch of asafoetida (optional)

1½ tsp cumin seeds

(continued on next page)

1   Put 3 tbsp of the oil into a wide, non-stick pan over a high heat. When the oil is hot and beginning to bubble, put in the bay leaves, cloves, cardamom pods, cinnamon and red chillies. Stir once or twice until the bay leaf starts to darken.

2   Quickly put in the chicken pieces in a single layer and brown on both sides. Remove and spread out on a plate, leaving the oil and spices behind. Take the pan briefly off the heat and put in the lentils, turmeric and 1.2 litres (2 pints) water. Put it back on a high heat and bring to a simmer. Cover partially and cook gently for 20 minutes.

3   Meanwhile, sprinkle ½ tsp salt, black pepper, ½ tsp of the garam masala and the lemon juice on both sides of the chicken pieces. Rub in and set aside. When the lentils have cooked for 20 minutes, put in the chicken and its juices, green beans and 1½ tsp salt. Stir and bring to a simmer. Cover, turn the heat to low and cook gently for another 20 minutes, stirring now and then.

4   Two minutes before this last 20 minutes is over, put the remaining 3 tbsp oil in a medium-sized frying pan set over a high heat. When the oil is hot and beginning to bubble, add the asafoetida if using and the cumin seeds. Ten seconds later, add the onions. Stir and fry until they turn brown at the edges.

5   Add the garlic. Stir and fry until the onion has turned brown. Add the ground cumin and coriander, 1 tsp garam masala, and chilli powder if using. Stir once. Put in the tomatoes, stir for 30 seconds and pour this mixture into the pan with the chicken and lentils. Stir and serve.

(continued from previous page)

115 g (4 oz) onions, peeled and cut
  into fine half-rings
2 cloves garlic, peeled and finely
  chopped
1 tsp ground cumin
1 tsp ground coriander
⅛–¼ tsp chilli powder (optional)
12 cherry tomatoes, cut into halves,
  crossways, or 140 g (5 oz) plain
  tomatoes, diced

NUTRITION

Each portion contains:

Energy: 480–720 calories

Fat: 18–27 g of which saturates 4–6 g

COOK'S TIP

If you leave out the chillies, this
is a perfect dish for children.
Asafoetida is used in small
quantities to give a kick to Indian
foods. For easy use, buy the
ground variety.

CHICKEN BREASTS BAKED WITH GREEN CHILLIES AND ONIONS

SERVES: 4   PREPARATION: 15 MINS   COOKING: 25 MINS

INGREDIENTS

For the sauce:

2 tbsp tomato purée

1 tbsp Dijon-type French mustard

1 tsp ground cumin

1 tsp garam masala

1 tbsp lemon juice

½ tsp salt

⅛–¼ tsp chilli powder

250 ml (8 fl oz) single cream

4 boned, skinned chicken breast
    halves (about 560 g/1¼ lb)

salt and freshly ground black pepper

4 tbsp vegetable oil

5 cm (2 in) cinnamon stick

6 cardamom pods

6 cloves

140 g (5 oz) onions, peeled and cut
    into half-rings

2.5 cm (1 in) piece fresh ginger,
    peeled and cut into fine slices,
    then into fine strips

(continued on next page)

1 Pre-heat the oven to 350°F/180°C/gas 4.

2 Put the tomato purée in a bowl. Add 1 tbsp water and mix. Add all the remaining ingredients for the sauce in the listed order, mixing as you go and set aside.

3 Spread out the chicken pieces. Salt and pepper them generously on both sides.

4 Put 3 tbsp of the oil into a non-stick frying pan and set over a high heat. When the oil is hot and beginning to bubble, put in the cinnamon, cardamom pods and cloves. Ten seconds later, put in the chicken in a single layer and brown lightly on both sides. Remove with a slotted spoon and place in an ovenproof dish in a single layer.

5 Put the onions, ginger and green chillies into the oil that remains in the frying pan. Stir and fry them until they are light brown in colour. Remove with a slotted spoon and spread evenly over the chicken pieces.

6 Add the remaining oil to the frying pan and let it heat up. Put in the mustard seeds. As soon as they pop – this takes just seconds – put in the garlic. Stir. As soon as it starts to brown, pour in the sauce. As soon as the sauce starts bubbling, pour it over the chicken without displacing the onion mixture. Place the ovenproof dish, uncovered, in the oven and bake for 25 minutes. Serve immediately.

(continued from previous page)

1–3 fresh, hot green chillies,
de-seeded and cut at a diagonal
into fine strips

½ tsp black or yellow mustard seeds

1 clove garlic, peeled and finely
chopped

NUTRITION

Each portion contains:

Energy: 410 calories

Fat: 29 g of which saturates 11 g

COOK'S TIP

This is a wonderful method for
cooking chicken breasts as they
remain tender and very juicy. Serve
Rice with Mushrooms and Mustard
Seeds (page 77) and Cauliflower
with Ginger, Garlic and Green
Chillies (page 64) as side dishes.

QUICK CHICKEN KORMA

SERVES: 4   PREPARATION: 10 MINS   COOKING: 25–30 MINS

INGREDIENTS

4 cm (1½ in) piece fresh ginger,
   peeled and coarsely chopped
5–6 cloves garlic, peeled and
   coarsely chopped
6 tbsp vegetable oil
3 bay leaves
5 cm (2 in) cinnamon stick
8 cardamom pods
4 cloves
¼ tsp black cumin seeds (or
   ordinary cumin seeds)
130 g (4½ oz) onions, peeled and
   finely chopped
1 tbsp ground coriander
1 tbsp ground cumin
3 tinned plum tomatoes, chopped
1.5 kg (3 lb) chicken pieces,
   skinned and cut into serving
   portions, off the bone
¼ –1 tsp chilli powder
¼ tsp salt
3 tbsp single cream

1   Put the ginger, garlic and 3 tbsp water into an electric blender. Blend until you have a smooth paste.

2   Put the oil in a wide frying pan or sauté pan and set over a high heat. When the oil is hot and beginning to bubble, put in the bay leaves, cinnamon, cardamom pods, cloves and cumin seeds. Stir once or twice and put in the onions. Stir and fry for about 3 minutes or until the onions turn slightly brown.

3   Put in the paste from the blender, and the ground coriander and cumin and fry for a minute. Put in the chopped tomatoes and fry for another minute.

4   Put in the chicken, chilli powder, salt and 250 ml (8 fl oz) water. Bring to the boil. Cover, turn the heat to medium and cook for 15 minutes, turning the chicken pieces over now and then. Remove the cover, add the cream and cook on a high heat for another 7–8 minutes or until the sauce has thickened. Stir gently as you do this. Serve immediately.

COOK'S TIP

For this recipe, a frying pan or sauté pan wide enough to hold all the chicken in a single layer will be of great help. This entire dish can be made a day ahead of time and refrigerated. It re-heats well.

NUTRITION

Each portion contains:
Energy: 640 calories
Fat: 34 g of which saturates 9 g

PRAWNS STEAMED WITH MUSTARD SEEDS

SERVES: 4 PREPARATION: 10 MINS

COOKING: 10 MINS, PLUS 10 MINS FOR MARINATING

INGREDIENTS

1½ tsp black mustard seeds

1 tbsp finely chopped onion

1 fresh, hot green chilli, de-seeded
and finely chopped

¼ tsp ground turmeric

⅓ tsp salt

¼ tsp chilli powder

3 tbsp mustard oil

450 g (1 lb) medium-sized,
uncooked, unpeeled prawns,
peeled, de-veined and washed
then drained (tails can be left
on for decoration, if you wish)

NUTRITION

Each portion contains:

Energy: 125 calories

Fat: 9 g of which saturates 1.5 g

1 Grind the mustard seeds coarsely in the container of a clean coffee grinder or other spice grinder. Put into a medium-sized stainless steel, ceramic or ovenproof-glass bowl. Add 1 tbsp water and mix. Add the onion, green chilli, turmeric, salt, chilli powder and oil. Mix again. Put in the prawns and mix. Cover with foil and set aside for 10 minutes as you get your steaming equipment ready.

There are two methods for steaming. Follow either step 2 or step 3.

2 Put the bowl of prawns into a large saucepan (the bowl should not touch the sides of the pan). Pour boiling water into the pan so that it comes one-third of the way up the side of the bowl. Cover the saucepan and steam.

3 Put water in the bottom third of a large wok. Bring to the boil. Put a bamboo or perforated metal steaming-tray on top of the water. Place the bowl of prawns on the tray, cover the wok and steam.

4 Steam, covered, for about 10 minutes or until the prawns just turn opaque all the way through. Stir the prawns once after about 6 minutes, covering the bowl and steaming utensil again afterwards.

COOK'S TIP

This dish is always eaten with plain rice. Mustard oil is sold by Indian grocers. Pungent when raw, it turns comfortingly sweet when heated. If you prefer, pieces of fresh haddock can be substituted for the prawns.

FISH FILLETS IN A 'CURRY' SAUCE

SERVES: 4–5   PREPARATION: 15 MINS

COOKING: 25 MINS, PLUS 15 MINS FOR MARINATING

INGREDIENTS

900 g (2 lb) thick fish fillet or
    fillets (see Cook's Tip), skin
    removed if possible
500 ml (18 fl oz) milk
1 tsp salt
lots of freshly ground black pepper
½ tsp chilli powder
¼ tsp ground turmeric
5 tbsp breadcrumbs
60 g (2 oz) unsalted butter
4 tbsp curry powder
2 tbsp plain flour
3 tbsp finely chopped green
    coriander, plus some whole
    leaves to garnish
2–3 tsp lemon juice

NUTRITION

Each portion contains:

Energy: 370–465 calories

Fat: 15–19 g of which saturates 9–11 g

1 Arrange a shelf in the upper third of the oven and pre-heat the oven to its highest temperature.

2 Spread the fish out in a deep dish. Combine the milk, salt, pepper, chilli powder and turmeric in a jug and pour over the fish. Set aside for 15 minutes. Lift the fish out of the milk and dust both sides with the breadcrumbs, patting them on so that they stick well. Reserve the milk. Put the fish in a shallow baking tray lined with foil. Dot with 30 g (1 oz) of the butter and bake for 15 minutes.

3 While the fish bakes, set the milk to heat in a small saucepan. Melt the remaining 30 g (1 oz) butter in a small, heavy saucepan over a medium-low heat. When it is melted and bubbling, put in the curry powder. Stir for a minute. Add the flour. Stir for about 2 minutes. It should keep bubbling.

4 Take the saucepan off the heat and, using a whisk, beat in the hot milk. Now put the saucepan on a medium-high heat and stir with the whisk until the sauce comes to the boil. Boil for a minute, whisking all the time. Add the green coriander and lemon juice and stir.

5 Put the fish on a serving plate and pour the sauce over the top.

COOK'S TIP

You may use any fish fillets. Cod, haddock and halibut are all fine, although fillets of dark, oily fish, such as blue fish and mackerel, are ideal.

SPICY GRILLED FISH

SERVES: 2–3   PREPARATION: 10 MINS

COOKING: 25 MINS, PLUS 10 MINS FOR MARINATING

INGREDIENTS

560 g (1¼ lb) fish such as a
    salmon trout, trout or small
    salmon, scaled, gutted, cleaned
    and left whole

salt

3 tbsp lemon juice

60 g (2 oz) onion, peeled and
    coarsely chopped

2 cloves garlic, peeled and coarsely
    chopped

2.5 cm (1 in) piece fresh ginger

1 fresh, hot green chilli, de-seeded
    and sliced

¼ tsp ground turmeric

1 tsp garam masala

¼ tsp chilli powder

175 ml (6 fl oz) tinned coconut
    milk, well stirred

a little vegetable oil

NUTRITION

Each portion contains:

Energy: 500–760 calories

Fat: 37–56 g of which saturates 14–21 g

1 Wash the fish well and pat dry. Cut 3–4 deep, diagonal slits across both sides of the fish. Rub with ½ tsp salt and 1 tbsp of the lemon juice. Set aside as you make the marinade.

2 Combine the remaining lemon juice, ¼ tsp salt, onion, garlic, ginger, chilli, turmeric, garam masala and chilli powder in a blender and blend until smooth. Empty the paste into a shallow dish large enough to hold the fish. Add the coconut milk and mix. Put the fish into the dish and rub with the marinade. Leave for 5–10 minutes.

3 Meanwhile, pre-heat the grill and oil the grill rack with a little vegetable oil. The rack should be placed about 15 cm (6 in) from the source of heat.

4 Lift the fish out of the marinade and place it on the rack. Grill for about 25 minutes, turning every 5 minutes and basting frequently with marinade. Turn once, midway through the cooking, using the flat side of a large knife. If the fish browns too fast, move it further away from the source of heat. Do not baste towards the end to allow the fish to form a crust. Serve immediately.

COOK'S TIP

A hinged wire holder helps the grilling as the fish can be turned and basted with ease. If you wish, you can garnish the fish with small whole chillies.

SPINACH WITH GINGER AND GREEN CHILLIES

SERVES: 4   PREPARATION: 5 MINS   COOKING: 10 MINS

INGREDIENTS

2 cm (1 in) piece fresh ginger,
  peeled
3 tbsp vegetable oil
500 g (18 oz) trimmed, washed
  spinach
2–3 fresh, hot green chillies,
  de-seeded and finely chopped
about ½ tsp salt
½ tsp garam masala
¼ tsp sugar
⅛ tsp chilli powder

NUTRITION

Each portion contains:
Energy: 100 calories
Fat: 9 g of which saturates 1 g

1 Cut the ginger, crossways, into thick slices. Stacking a few slices at a time together, cut them into fine slivers.

2 Put the oil in a wok or large, wide pan and set over a high heat. When the oil is hot and beginning to bubble, put in the ginger. Stir until the ginger starts to brown.

3 Put in the spinach and chillies. Stir and cook until the spinach has wilted completely. Add the remaining ingredients. Stir and cook for another 5 minutes. Serve immediately.

COOK'S TIP

Indians tend to eat a lot of greens, sometimes a single variety by itself, sometimes mixed with other leaves. The most commonly available of all greens in the West is spinach and that is what I have used here. I keep the leaves whole, but if they are very large you might need to chop them coarsely. This recipe is ideal to serve with blander dishes.

STIR-FRIED GREEN CABBAGE WITH FENNEL SEEDS

SERVES: 4 PREPARATION: 5 MINS COOKING: 18 MINS

INGREDIENTS

675 g (1½ lb) green cabbage (half
   a big head)
4 tbsp vegetable oil
¾ tsp cumin seeds
½ tsp fennel seeds
1 tsp sesame seeds
200 g (7 oz) onions, peeled and cut
   lengthways, into fine half-rings
1 tsp salt
⅛ –¼ tsp chilli powder
1 tbsp lemon juice
½ tsp garam masala

NUTRITION

Each portion contains:
Energy: 160 calories
Fat: 11 g of which saturates 2 g

1 Remove the coarse outer leaves of the cabbage. If you have a cabbage half, cut it in half again, lengthways, and then core the sections. Now cut each section, lengthways, into very fine, long shreds. A bread knife is ideal for this. (You could also use a food processor.)

2 Put the oil in a wide, preferably non-stick, pan and set over a highish heat. When the oil is hot and beginning to bubble, put in the cumin, fennel and sesame seeds. As soon as the sesame seeds begin to pop, put in the onions. Stir and fry for 3–4 minutes or until the onions start to turn brown.

3 Add the cabbage. Stir and fry for about 6 minutes or until the cabbage too has browned somewhat.

4 Add the salt and chilli powder. Turn the heat down to medium-low and cook, stirring now and then, for another 7–8 minutes or until the onions appear caramelized and soft. Add the lemon juice and garam masala. Stir to mix and serve immediately.

COOK'S TIP

The cabbage and onions get nicely browned here and taste gloriously of fennel. You could easily serve this with Western-style sausages, hams, pork chops or any kind of roast pork meat, or try it with roast lamb or even duck and venison.

CAULIFLOWER WITH GINGER, GARLIC AND GREEN CHILLIES

SERVES: 3–4   PREPARATION: 10 MINS   COOKING: 7–9 MINS

INGREDIENTS

3 tbsp vegetable oil

½ tsp cumin seeds

½ tsp yellow mustard seeds

3 cloves garlic, peeled and finely
   chopped

2.5 cm (1 in) piece fresh ginger,
   peeled and cut into fine shreds

450 g (1 lb) cauliflower florets

1–3 fresh, hot green chillies,
   de-seeded and chopped

¾ tsp salt

freshly ground black pepper

½ tsp garam masala

⅛ tsp chilli powder or to taste

NUTRITION

Each portion contains:

Energy: 112–150 calories

Fat: 9–12 g of which saturates 1.5–2 g

1   Put the oil in a wok or a large, wide pan with a lid and set over a highish heat. When the oil is hot and beginning to bubble, put in the cumin and mustard seeds. As soon as the mustard seeds begin to pop – this takes just a few seconds – put in the garlic, ginger, cauliflower and green chillies, all at the same time. Stir and fry for about 5–7 minutes or until the cauliflower has begun to turn brown.

2   Now put in the salt, black pepper, garam masala and chilli powder and give the cauliflower florets a good toss. Put in 4 tbsp water and cover the wok or pan immediately. Cook for 2 minutes more and serve straight away.

COOK'S TIP

This is a simple, everyday dish. The special taste comes from allowing the florets to brown slightly. Do not cut them too small or they might fall apart.

RED LENTILS 'TARKA'

SERVES: 6–8   PREPARATION: 5 MINS   COOKING: 35–40 MINS

INGREDIENTS

340 g (12 oz) red lentils (masoor
    dal)
½ tsp ground turmeric
1¼–1½ tsp salt
3 tbsp vegetable oil or ghee
generous pinch of ground asafoetida
1 tsp cumin seeds
3–5 dried, hot red chillies

NUTRITION

Each portion contains:

Energy: 170–230 calories

Fat: 5–6 g of which saturates 0.7–1 g

1 Pick over the lentils and wash in several changes of water. Drain. Put in a heavy saucepan. Add 1.2 litres (2 pints) water and the turmeric. Stir and bring to a simmer. (Do not let it boil over.)

2 Cover in such a way as to leave the lid just very slightly ajar, turn the heat to low and simmer gently for 35–40 minutes or until tender. Stir a few times during the cooking. Add the salt and mix. Leave covered, on very low heat, as you do the next step.

3 Put the oil in a small frying pan and set over a highish heat. When the oil is hot and beginning to bubble, put in the asafoetida then, a second later, the cumin seeds. Let the cumin sizzle for a few seconds.

4 Add the red chillies. As soon as they turn dark red (this takes just a few seconds), lift up the lid of the lentil pan and pour in the contents of the frying pan, oil as well as spices. Cover the saucepan immediately to trap the aromas. Warm through, stir and serve.

COOK'S TIP

Indians eat protein-rich legumes with many meals. Often, these are prepared with a flavouring, or 'tarka', of whole cumin seeds, asafoetida and whole chillies in hot oil or ghee. Mustard seeds and a choice of garlic, curry leaves, onions or tomatoes may be added to this. I have used red lentils because they cook faster than most traditional dals. Asafoetida is used in small quantities to give a kick to Indian foods. For easy use, buy the ground variety. Ghee is a butter that has been clarified so thoroughly that you can deep-fry in it. All Indian grocers sell it. Serve this dish with plain rice and a simple meat or vegetable.

WHOLE GREEN LENTILS WITH GREEN CORIANDER AND MINT

SERVES: 4   PREPARATION: 5 MINS   COOKING: 20 MINS

INGREDIENTS

3 tbsp vegetable oil

½ tsp cumin seeds

½ tsp black or yellow mustard seeds

pinch of ground asafoetida
   (optional)

1–3 dried, hot red chillies

115 g (4 oz) onions, peeled and cut
   into fine half-rings

2 cloves garlic, peeled and chopped

1 medium-sized tomato, chopped

180 g (6 oz) whole green lentils

¾ tsp salt

1 tsp ground coriander

2 tbsp chopped green coriander

2 tbsp chopped fresh mint, plus
   some whole leaves to garnish

NUTRITION

Each portion contains:

Energy: 222 calories

Fat: 9 g of which saturates 1 g

1   Put the oil in a pressure-cooker and set over a highish heat. When the oil is hot and beginning to bubble, put in the cumin and mustard seeds. As soon as the mustard seeds begin to pop – this takes just a few seconds – put in the asafoetida, if using, and the red chillies. Stir once.

2   Put in the onions, garlic and tomato. Stir for about 2 minutes or until the onions brown slightly.

3   Now put in the lentils, 800 ml (1 pint 7 fl oz) water, salt, ground coriander, green coriander and mint. Stir and bring to a simmer. Cover, turn the heat to high and bring up to pressure. Turn the heat down to low and cook at full pressure for 15 minutes. Take off the heat, reduce the pressure with cool water and serve, garnished with whole mint leaves.

COOK'S TIP

For speed, I use a pressure-cooker although you could cook the lentils in an ordinary saucepan for 50–60 minutes. You would need to increase the water by 300 ml (10 fl oz). If you cannot get fresh mint, use more green coriander.

MUSHROOM CURRY

SERVES: 4 PREPARATION: 10 MINS COOKING: 15 MINS

INGREDIENTS

4 cm (1½ in) piece fresh ginger,
  peeled and chopped

115 g (4 oz) onions, peeled and
  chopped

3 cloves garlic, peeled and chopped

6 tbsp vegetable oil

450 g (1 lb) large mushrooms, cut
  into large, chunky pieces

3 tbsp natural yoghurt

1 tsp tomato purée

2 tsp ground coriander

¾ tsp salt

⅛–¼ tsp chilli powder

2 tbsp chopped green coriander

NUTRITION

Each portion contains:

Energy: 180 calories

Fat: 17 g of which saturates 2.5 g

1 Put the ginger, onion and garlic into a blender along with 3 tbsp water and blend until smooth.

2 Put 3 tbsp of the oil in a non-stick frying pan and set over a high heat. When the oil is hot and beginning to bubble, put in the mushrooms. Stir and fry for 2–3 minutes or until the mushrooms have lost their raw look. Empty the contents of the pan into a bowl. Wipe the pan.

3 Put the remaining 3 tbsp oil into the pan and set over a high heat. When the oil is hot and beginning to bubble, put in the paste from the blender. Stir and fry for 3–4 minutes until it starts turning brown. Add 1 tbsp of the yoghurt and fry for 30 seconds. Add another tbsp of the yoghurt and fry for 30 seconds. Do this a third time.

4 Now put in the tomato purée and fry for 30 seconds. Put in the ground coriander and stir once or twice. Now put in 300 ml (10 fl oz) water, the mushrooms and their juices, salt and chilli powder. Stir and bring to a simmer. Turn the heat to low and simmer for 5 minutes. Sprinkle the green coriander over the top and serve immediately.

NEW POTATOES WITH CUMIN

SERVES: 4–6   PREPARATION: 10 MINS   COOKING: 20 MINS

INGREDIENTS

900 g (2 lb) new potatoes

salt

2½ tbsp vegetable oil

1 tsp cumin seeds

1 tsp ground cumin

½ tsp garam masala

⅛–¼ tsp chilli powder

2–3 tbsp chopped green coriander

NUTRITION

Each portion contains:

Energy: 142–215 calories

Fat: 5–7 g of which saturates 0.7–1 g

1 Scrub the potatoes and put them in a saucepan. Cover with water to come about 2.5 cm (1 in) above the potatoes. Add 1 tbsp salt to the water and bring to the boil. Cover. Boil until the potatoes are just tender. Drain and peel when cool.

2 Put the oil in a large frying pan and set over a medium-high heat. When the oil is hot and beginning to bubble, add the cumin seeds and let them sizzle for a few seconds.

3 Now put in the potatoes. Turn the heat down to medium. Brown the potatoes lightly on all sides. Turn the heat to low and add ¼ tsp salt and the ground cumin, garam masala and chilli powder. Cook, stirring, for a minute.

4 Add the green coriander, toss to mix and serve immediately.

COOK'S TIP

Here is one of my favourite ways of preparing new potatoes, Indian-style. You may serve them with an Indian meal or, if you like, with Western dishes – anything from roasts to sausages.

TURMERIC RICE

SERVES: 4–6   PREPARATION: 5 MINS   COOKING: 25 MINS

INGREDIENTS

450 g (1 lb) basmati or long-grain
  rice

3 tbsp vegetable oil

3 cloves

1 bay leaf

4 cardamom pods

2.5 cm (1 in) cinnamon stick

2 cloves garlic, peeled and finely
  chopped

¼ tsp ground turmeric

1 tsp salt

2 tbsp finely sliced chives or the
  green part of spring onions

NUTRITION

Each portion contains:

Energy: 320–480 calories

Fat: 6–9 g of which saturates 0.8–1 g

1 Put the rice in a bowl and wash well in several changes of water. Drain and leave in a strainer set over a bowl.

2 Put the oil in a heavy saucepan and set over a medium-high heat. When the oil is hot and beginning to bubble, put in the cloves, bay leaf, cardamom pods and cinnamon. Stir once or twice and put in the garlic.

3 As soon as the garlic turns medium-brown, put in the rice, turmeric and salt. Stir gently for a minute. Now put in 675 ml (22 fl oz) water and bring to the boil. Cover tightly, turn the heat down to very, very low and cook for 25 minutes. Stir the rice with a fork or rice serverto separate the grains and serve immediately.

COOK'S TIP

This yellow, lightly seasoned rice
may be served with almost any
Indian meal.

BASMATI RICE WITH SPICES AND SAFFRON

SERVES: 6 PREPARATION: 10 MINS, PLUS SOAKING TIME

COOKING: 30 MINS

INGREDIENTS

1 tsp saffron threads

2 tbsp warm milk

350 g (12 oz) basmati or long-grain
    rice

salt

2 tbsp vegetable oil

5 cardamom pods

two 7.5 cm (3 in) cinnamon sticks

NUTRITION

Each portion contains:

Energy: 250 calories

Fat: 4 g of which saturates 0.5 g

COOK'S TIP

Although this recipe calls for
basmati, any long-grain, fine-
quality rice can be used instead.

---

1 Dry-roast the saffron in a heavy-based frying pan, cool slightly, then crumble into the warm milk and leave to soak for about 30 minutes.

2 Put the rice in a bowl and wash well in several changes of cold water. Fill the bowl with 1.1 litres (2 pints) fresh water, add ½ tsp salt and leave to soak for 30 minutes. Drain.

3 Heat the oil in a heavy-based pan or cooking pot over a medium heat. Put in the cardamom pods and cinnamon sticks, and stir over the heat a few times. Add the rice and fry, stirring, for about 1 minute.

4 Add 550 ml (18 fl oz) water and ¾ tsp salt. Bring to the boil, cover with a tight-fitting lid, reduce the heat to very low and cook for 20 minutes.

5 Gently but quickly fork through the rice to separate the grains. Drizzle the saffron-infused milk over the rice to form streaks of colour. Re-cover and cook for a further 10 minutes or until the rice is tender. Turn the rice onto a serving platter using a fork to separate the grains. Serve at once.

See full picture on page 78

RICE WITH MUSHROOMS AND MUSTARD SEEDS

SERVES: 4–5   PREPARATION: 10 MINS   COOKING: 25 MINS

INGREDIENTS

450 g (1 lb) long-grain rice

3 tbsp vegetable oil

½ tsp cumin seeds

½ tsp black or yellow mustard seeds

30 g (1 oz) onion, peeled and cut
    into fine half-rings

10 medium-sized mushrooms, sliced
    lengthways

675 ml (22 fl oz) chicken stock or
    water

salt

NUTRITION

Each portion contains:

Energy: 390–490 calories

Fat: 7–9 g of which saturates 0.8–1 g

1   Put the rice in a bowl and wash well in several changes of water.
    Drain and leave in a strainer set over a bowl.

2   Put the oil in a heavy-based saucepan and set over a medium-high
    heat. When the oil is hot and beginning to bubble, put in the cumin
    and mustard seeds. As soon as the mustard seeds begin to pop – this
    takes just a few seconds – put in the onion. Stir and fry until the
    onion browns a little. Put in the mushrooms and stir for a minute.

3   Now put in the drained rice and stir for a minute. Put in the stock
    and about ½ tsp salt if your stock is salted, 1 tsp salt if you are
    using water or unsalted stock. Bring to the boil. Cover tightly, turn
    the heat to very, very low and cook for 25 minutes. Stir with a fork to
    separate the grains and serve immediately.

COOK'S TIP
Almost any variety of fresh,
seasonal mushrooms may be used

See full picture on page 79

DESSERTS
and drinks

CARAMELIZED CARDAMOM APPLES WITH PISTACHIO CREAM

SERVES: 4   PREPARATION: 10 MINS   COOKING: 15 MINS

INGREDIENTS

For the cream:

250 ml (8 fl oz) double cream for whipping

2 tbsp pistachios, finely chopped

115 g (4 oz) unsalted butter

4 medium-sized sour, firm apples

¼ tsp finely ground cardamom seeds

⅛ tsp ground cinnamon

⅛ tsp ground cloves

140 g (5 oz) sugar

3 tbsp blanched, slivered almonds

2 tbsp chopped walnuts

NUTRITION

Each portion contains:

Energy: 787 calories

Fat: 67 g of which saturates 35 g

1 Whip the cream lightly until it just holds its shape but is not stiff at all. Fold half of the pistachio nuts into the cream. Refrigerate the cream.

2 Melt the butter over a low heat in a large, non-stick frying pan. Take the pan off the heat.

3 Peel, core and slice the apples thickly, dropping the slices into the butter as you cut them. Fold them into the butter as you go so that they do not discolour. (You could, if you like, keep the frying pan over very low heat as you do this.)

4 Add the cardamom, cinnamon, cloves, sugar, almonds and walnuts. Cook on a medium heat for 2–3 minutes, stirring gently as you do so. Now turn the heat to high. Cook for 8–10 minutes, stirring very gently now and then, until the apples have caramelized lightly.

5 Serve on individual plates with a dollop of the cream over the apples. Sprinkle the remaining chopped pistachios over the cream.

COOK'S TIP

This is an easy dessert that can be made with any sour, firm apples such as Bramleys or Granny Smiths. It may be served hot or warm.

PALE GREEN SPICY, MINTY LASSI

SERVES: 2   PREPARATION: 5 MINS

INGREDIENTS

300 ml (10 fl oz) natural yoghurt

3 tbsp chopped green coriander

25 large mint leaves or 30 small
   ones

1 cm (½ in) piece fresh ginger,
   peeled and chopped

½ fresh, hot green chilli,
   de-seeded and coarsely chopped

⅓ tsp salt or to taste

¼ tsp ground roasted cumin seeds
   (optional)

8 ice cubes

1 Simply combine all the ingredients in an electric blender and blend until smooth. Some ice pieces may remain. Pour into 2 glasses and serve immediately.

NUTRITION

Each portion contains:

Energy: 120 calories

Fat: 4 g of which saturates 2.5 g

COOK'S TIP

I cannot think of anything more refreshing on a hot summer day. Use the upper half of the chilli for more heat, the lower part for less.

SWEET, PALE ORANGE MANGO LASSI

SERVES: 2−3   PREPARATION: 5 MINS

INGREDIENTS

300 ml (10 fl oz) natural yoghurt

250 ml (8 fl oz) chopped, ripe
   mango flesh

3 tbsp sugar, or to taste

¼ tsp ground cardamom seeds

8 ice cubes

1 Combine all the ingredients in an electric blender and blend. Some ice pieces may remain. Pour into 2-3 glasses and serve.

NUTRITION

Each portion contains:

Energy: 185–280 calories

Fat: 3–5 g of which saturates 2-3 g

COOK'S TIP

This could be made with the peeled flesh of fresh ripe mangoes or with good tinned ones. Drain the tinned mangoes before using them.

PEARS POACHED IN SAFFRON SYRUP

SERVES: 4–8   PREPARATION: 10 MINS   COOKING: 20–25 MINS

INGREDIENTS

200 g (7 oz) sugar

6 whole cardamom pods

¼ tsp saffron threads

3 tbsp lemon juice

4 firm pears

NUTRITION

Each portion contains:

Energy: 130–260 calories

Fat: 0 g of which saturates 0 g

1 Put the sugar into a medium-sized heavy-based saucepan with 450 ml (¾ pint) water. Add the cardamom pods, saffron and lemon juice. Heat gently until the sugar dissolves, then bring to a simmer.

2 Peel the pears, halve lengthways and remove the core; add each pear to the simmering syrup as soon it is cut, to avoid discoloration. Cover and cook gently for 20–25 minutes, turning the pears in the syrup from time to time.

3 Carefully lift the pears out of the liquid and arrange them in a serving dish in a single layer, cut-side down. Boil the syrup until it is reduced to about 250 ml (8 fl oz) and thickened slightly. Pour the reduced syrup evenly over the pears. Allow to cool before serving.

COOK'S TIP

These pears, which I first made with the purest saffron from Kashmir, are heavenly. They turn a rich gold colour and are suffused with the heady aromas of saffron and cardamom – amongst the most prized spices in the world.

RICE PUDDING WITH CARDAMOM AND PISTACHIOS

SERVES: 4   PREPARATION: 10 MINS   COOKING: 1¼ HOURS

INGREDIENTS

1.1 litres (2 pints) milk

2 tbsp long-grain rice

4 whole cardamom pods, bruised

2 tbsp sugar

10 unsalted pistachio nuts, slivered

extra pistachio nuts, to decorate

NUTRITION

Each portion contains:

Energy: 300 calories

Fat: 18 g of which saturates 7 g

1 Combine the milk, rice and cardamom pods in a heavy-based pan or cooking pot. Slowly bring to the boil. Lower the heat and simmer steadily until the milk is reduced to approximately 600 ml (1 pint); this should take about 1¼ hours. Turn off the heat.

2 Remove and discard the cardamom pods. Add the sugar and pistachio nuts, stir well, then leave to cool.

3 Stir the rice again. Pour into a serving bowl. Sprinkle a few more slivered pistachios on top. Cover and refrigerate until ready to serve.

COOK'S TIP

This is my mother's recipe for rice pudding (or kheer), which she set in shallow half-baked earthenware bowls called shakoras. You could serve your kheer in individual custard bowls or pots.

For full picture see page 91

BANANA HALVA

SERVES: 2–4   PREPARATION: 10 MINS   COOKING: 16 MINS

INGREDIENTS

4 very ripe bananas

1 tbsp vegetable oil

2 tbsp sugar

1 tbsp chopped unsalted, peeled
    pistachios

½ tbsp chopped walnuts

4 tbsp lightly whipped double cream
    or clotted cream

NUTRITION

Each portion contains:

Energy: 200–400 calories

Fat: 18–18 g of which saturates 2–4 g

1 Peel the bananas and mash them.

2 Put the oil in a non-stick frying pan and set over a highish heat. When the oil is hot and beginning to bubble, put in the mashed bananas. Stir and fry for 5–6 minutes. Turn the heat to medium and stir and fry for another 10 minutes or until the bananas have browned and turned to a kind of soft toffee.

3 Turn the heat to low. Add the sugar. Stir for another 30 seconds or until the sugar has dissolved. Add the pistachios and walnuts and mix in. Cool to room temperature, then spoon into a bowl and cover with cling film until serving time. Cut or mould the halva into shapes (see Cook's Tip). Serve with whipped or clotted cream.

COOK'S TIP

If you love bananas in all forms, you will love this simple but unusual preparation. I often form the halva, which is quite malleable, into fig shapes and serve it on individual plates with whipped cream. The halva will keep, unrefrigerated, for a couple of days. Just wrap it well in cling film.

For full picture see page 90